How to Spot and Invest

Logan Evans

Copyright Page

First edition
All Rights Reserved
Author: © 2024, Logan Evans

Index

Why Your Money Should Work For You

From the time we are young children, we are often taught that in order to earn money we have to work hard, spend long hours at the office, or exert ourselves physically to earn a salary. While that is a valid way to earn income, it is not the only way. The reality is that if you want to build a financially solid life and have the freedom to enjoy your time, you cannot rely on your day job alone. At some point, the money you earn needs to start working for you, not the other way around. This idea may sound abstract at first, but it is quite simple: instead of constantly trading your time for money, you need to put that money to work to make more money on its own.

Imagine that every bill you have is like an employee. If you keep it in a box or in the bank doing nothing, it just sits there, motionless, without fulfilling any function. But, if you decide to invest it wisely, it's like hiring it to do a job. Now, instead of sitting somewhere with no purpose, that money slowly starts multiplying, earning interest, increasing in value, or generating passive income for you. The key is to understand that money has enormous potential when you use it as a tool, not just a means to pay bills or buy things.

Putting your money to work doesn't mean you'll automatically become a millionaire overnight. Rather, it's a long-term process where your savings and financial resources become a driving force that moves you toward your goals. Think of it like planting a seed: at first, it may seem like nothing is happening. You water the plant, you take care of it, and the growth may be so slow that you get impatient. However, over time, that seed grows into a strong, robust tree that bears fruit. The same goes for well-thought-out investments: at first it may seem like the results are minimal, but with patience and perseverance, the fruits come.

The great benefit of making your money work for you is that it frees up your time. Have you noticed that the richest people in the world aren't working 24 hours a day? This isn't because they're smarter than everyone else, but because they've learned to use their money as a powerful tool. While you're sleeping, that money can be generating income through investments in real estate, stocks, businesses, or any other vehicle that produces value over time. This concept, called passive income, means you can receive money regularly without having to be present or actively work hard to earn it.

Not making your money work for you is like owning a luxury car and never using it. You might be excited about owning it, but if you don't put it to work, it doesn't serve its purpose. On the other hand, when you decide to invest, you're taking advantage of that car's full potential, taking it on paths that bring you closer to your goals. And here's something important: you don't need to be a millionaire to start investing. Even small amounts of money can turn into large sums if you invest them consistently and give them time to grow.

Plus, when money works for you, you're building a shield against uncertainty. Life is unpredictable, and relying solely on a paycheck can put you in a vulnerable position if you lose your job or have an emergency. By investing, you're creating multiple streams of income that can keep you afloat even in tough times. It's like building a financial safety net that protects you when you need it most.

It's important to clarify that it's not just about saving. Saving is a good first step, but it's not enough. If you leave your money in a traditional bank account, the growth will be minimal, and inflation can even cause it to lose value over time. Investing, on the other hand, is taking that saved money and placing it in options that make it grow, whether in financial markets, in your own business, or in tangible assets such as property.

So why is it so important to have your money work for you? Because it gives you freedom. Freedom to choose how you want to live your life, to decide what you want to spend your time on, and to enjoy more of the things that really matter. Instead of spending your entire life running after money, you make money run to you. It's a way to break the cycle of working just to survive and start building a more fulfilling and meaningful life.

If you start to see money as an ally instead of a limited resource, you will realize that every financial decision you make can bring you closer or further away from that freedom. Learn to make smart decisions, look for opportunities that allow you to put your resources to work, and watch how little by little your financial situation transforms. It is a change that requires patience and dedication, but the results are worth it. And the best of all is that you have the control to start today.

The Psychology of the Investor

Investing is not just about numbers, charts or financial strategies; it is also a mental game in which your thoughts, emotions and beliefs play a crucial role. Investor psychology is one of the most determining factors for success or failure in the world of investments. You can have all the technical knowledge in the world, but if you do not know how to control your emotions and understand your way of thinking, you can make decisions that lead directly to unnecessary losses.

Fear is one of an investor's biggest enemies. It's natural to feel afraid of losing money, especially when you've worked hard to earn it. This fear can lead to impulsive decisions, such as selling an investment too soon just because its value temporarily dropped. However, fluctuations are normal in most investments, especially in markets like stocks or cryptocurrencies. Successful investors understand that not every decline means a loss, and they have the patience to wait for prices to recover, if the fundamentals of the investment are solid.

On the other hand, there is greed, which is the opposite side of fear, but just as dangerous. When an investment starts to rise rapidly, it is easy to fall into the trap of wanting more. This desire can lead you to ignore clear signs that it is time to sell or to invest too much in something that seems promising, but is actually a bubble. Greed can also push you to follow trends without doing deep analysis, just because everyone is talking about it. Many have lost fortunes because they acted with excessive enthusiasm, without evaluating the real risks.

An important aspect of investor psychology is accepting that you won't always be right. Sometimes, you'll invest in something that looked promising and lose money. That doesn't mean you're a bad investor, but how you handle that loss does define how far you can go. The best investors view losses as lessons. They analyze what went wrong, learn from the experience, and use that knowledge to make better decisions in the future. If you dwell on a loss and let it affect your future decisions, you'll be sabotaging yourself.

Patience is another key virtue in investor psychology. We live in a world that wants quick results, but the best investments often take time to mature. This can be difficult when you see others seem to be making quick money with riskier moves, but remember that sustainable success is rarely immediate. Having patience means trusting your analysis and strategy, even when the results aren't immediate.

In addition to patience, discipline is key. Investing without a plan is like sailing aimlessly: you can end up lost or in the wrong place. Before you put your money into any opportunity, you need to set clear rules for yourself. Decide how much you are willing to risk, when it is time to buy or sell, and make sure you stick to that plan, even when your emotions try to convince you otherwise. Discipline protects you from making impulsive decisions that can be costly.

Another important element is the ability to manage stress. Investing, especially in volatile markets, can be stressful. Prices go up and down, news can be alarming, and sometimes it seems like everything is against you. If you don't know how to manage that stress, you may make hasty decisions or feel overwhelmed to the point of avoiding any action. Techniques such as meditation, physical exercise, or simply temporarily disconnecting from the market noise can help you stay calm.

Investor psychology also involves having an open and adaptable mindset. Markets are constantly changing, and what worked yesterday may not work tomorrow. Investors who stick to one strategy without adapting often get left behind. This doesn't mean you should change course with every new trend, but you should be willing to reevaluate your methods and learn new things.

A common mistake is comparing yourself to others. It's easy to fall into the trap of measuring your success based on what others are achieving, especially when social media is full of people showing off their apparent financial successes. But every investor has a unique path, and comparing your results to others only breeds frustration and insecurity. Instead, focus on your own goals and how you can improve yourself.

Finally, remember that investing should be a rational process, not an emotional one. Every decision should be based on analysis and hard data, not hunches or hearsay. This doesn't mean you should never follow your intuition, but that intuition should be backed up by solid information. If you manage to maintain a rational and consistent approach, you'll have a huge advantage over many other investors.

Investor psychology isn't something you master overnight. It requires practice, self-awareness, and a constant effort to improve. But once you understand and control your emotions and thought patterns, you're much more prepared to make sound decisions and build a solid path to financial success. Investing isn't just a numbers game, it's a reflection of your mindset and how you choose to approach the world.

Knowing the Terrain

Before you venture into the world of investing, it's essential to know the terrain you're going into. Imagine you're going to explore a jungle. What would you do before you set off? You'd probably look for a map, information about the weather, the animals you might encounter, and even the safest routes to avoid danger. Investing works the same way. You can't just go in blindly and hope for the best. You need to prepare yourself, understand the rules of the game, and familiarize yourself with the different scenarios you might face.

The investment landscape is full of options, each with its own characteristics, risks and rewards. Some paths are safer but slower to move, such as bonds or certificates of deposit. Others may be riskier but offer big rewards, such as stocks in tech startups or the cryptocurrency market. To make smart choices, you first need to understand what those options are and how they work. Not every investment is for everyone, and that's okay. The important thing is to know which one best fits your goals and risk tolerance.

Knowing the terrain also means learning about the risks involved. All investments have some degree of risk, even the safest ones. For example, if you choose to invest in real estate, there are risks associated with changes in the market, problems with tenants, or even natural disasters. If you choose to invest in stocks, risks can come from market volatility, company performance, or global economic events. The key is to not let yourself be paralyzed by fear, but to be prepared to face them. Researching and planning helps you reduce unpleasant surprises.

Furthermore, each type of investment has its own language, and understanding it is part of knowing the terrain. Terms like dividends, yields, volatility or diversification may sound complicated at first, but they are not so much once you understand them. For example, diversification is simply not putting all your eggs in one basket. By investing in different assets, sectors or markets, you reduce the risk that a bad decision will affect your entire portfolio. Familiarizing yourself with these concepts is like learning to read the map before starting your adventure.

Another crucial aspect of knowing your terrain is understanding the economic and political context. Markets don't exist in a vacuum; they are influenced by a variety of external factors. If there is an economic downturn, certain sectors are likely to suffer more than others. If a country is in political strife, investments related to that location may be more volatile. Staying informed about what is happening in the world gives you an advantage in anticipating potential changes and adjusting your strategies accordingly.

You also need to know the players on the ground. Who are the companies, institutions or people behind the investments you are considering? For example, if you plan to invest in stocks, it is important to research the company: its track record, its products, its competitors and its leadership. If you decide to invest in managed funds, make sure you understand who runs those funds and what their strategies are. Knowing the players allows you to make decisions based on data and not hunches.

Knowing the terrain also means being honest with yourself. What is your current financial situation? How much can you afford to invest without compromising your basic needs? How long can you wait to see results? These questions are essential because not all investments are suitable for all people. If you need immediate liquidity, real estate is probably not the best option for you. If you have a low risk tolerance, you may prefer more conservative options such as bonds.

Finally, exploring the terrain also means learning from those who have already done it. There are endless resources available: books, courses, blogs, forums, and even professional financial advisors. Taking advantage of these tools allows you to gain knowledge without having to learn everything by trial and error. Listening to the experiences of others can help you avoid common mistakes and identify opportunities you may not have considered.

Learning the ropes isn't something you do once. It's an ongoing process. The investment world is constantly changing, and what's true today may not be true tomorrow. That's why you must always stay in learning mode, updating your knowledge and adjusting your strategies as needed. This commitment to learning is what separates successful investors from those who simply wing it.

In short, entering the world of investing without knowing the terrain is like walking blindly down an unfamiliar path. You might get lucky and reach your destination, but you're just as likely to end up lost or hurt. Taking the time to understand the environment, the risks, the opportunities, and your own capabilities puts you in a much stronger position to make sound decisions. And the best part is that this preparation not only gives you confidence, it makes the whole experience more exciting and fulfilling. When you know the terrain, you become a prepared explorer, ready to take advantage of every opportunity that comes your way.

How to Analyze an Opportunity

Knowing how to analyse an opportunity is essential for anyone who wants to invest intelligently. No matter if you are considering buying a property, shares in a company, a business of your own or even a small project, the process should always start with a detailed evaluation. This means looking beyond the superficial, understanding the risks and benefits and making decisions based on data, not impulses or emotions. Below, I will explain how to do it step by step.

The first step in analyzing an opportunity is to understand exactly what it is. Often, an investment may seem promising at first glance because someone is enthusiastically describing it or because everyone is talking about it. But before you get excited, you need to ask yourself key questions. What is this opportunity? How does it create value or benefits? What problem does it solve or what need does it meet? If you can't answer these questions clearly, it's a sign that you need to do more research.

The next step is to thoroughly investigate the source of the opportunity. For example, if you are considering investing in a company, you should study its track record, its products or services, its position in the market, and who the people running it are. If it is a new business, you should investigate whether they have experience in the sector, what their plan is for growth, and how solid their initial numbers are. Knowing who is behind the opportunity will help you determine whether you can trust them and whether they are prepared to deliver on the promises they make.

A fundamental analysis for any investment opportunity is to look at the numbers. This may sound complicated, but it's really a matter of looking at a few essential things. If it's a business, look at its revenue, expenses, profits and debt. If it's a property, look at the price, maintenance costs, taxes and profitability potential. The key is to ask yourself if the numbers make sense and if they show a clear path to real profits. If the numbers are confusing or overly optimistic, be wary. A good opportunity must have a solid financial foundation.

Another crucial aspect is identifying risks. All opportunities, even the best ones, have risks. That's why part of your analysis should be to identify what these risks are and evaluate whether you are willing to take them. For example, a startup could fail due to competition or a lack of experience among its team. A property in a high-risk area for natural disasters could depreciate over time. Once you identify the risks, you need to evaluate how they could affect you and whether you have a plan to minimize or address them.

Forward-looking is also essential when analyzing an opportunity. Ask yourself how that investment might evolve in the coming years. If it's a business, does it have room to grow in the market? If it's a property, does the area it's located in have development potential or is it likely to lose value? Assessing the future involves looking at market trends, industry changes, and any external factors that may impact the success of the opportunity.

It's also important to understand what your role is in the investment. Some opportunities require you to be an active participant, such as running a business or overseeing a property. Others are more passive, such as investing in stocks and letting the market do its work. Ask yourself how much time, effort, and energy you are willing to put into this opportunity. If it requires more than you are willing to give, it may not be the best option for you.

Comparing options to other options is also a useful technique for analyzing an opportunity. Don't rush into a decision just because something looks interesting. Spend time researching similar options. For example, if you're considering investing in a property, look at other properties in the same area to compare prices and benefits. If it's a business, look at other companies in the same sector. This will give you a better idea of whether the opportunity you're evaluating is really worthwhile.

Another important point is to consider how well the opportunity fits with your personal and financial goals. If you are looking for stable, long-term income, a volatile investment like cryptocurrencies may not be the best option for you. If you want something with greater liquidity, a long-term project like real estate may not meet your immediate needs. Analyze whether the opportunity is aligned with what you are looking for, not just with what it promises.

Finally, don't underestimate the power of seeking advice. Talking to experts, mentors, or people who have experience in the type of investment you're considering can provide valuable insights. Often, they can see risks or benefits you hadn't considered. Also, make sure you understand all the technical or contractual language surrounding the opportunity. If something isn't clear, don't hesitate to ask questions until you fully understand.

In short, analyzing an opportunity is not about following your intuition or simply trusting what others say. It is a detailed process that requires time, research, and reflection. When you make decisions based on solid analysis, you reduce the likelihood of mistakes and increase your chances of success. So, before you jump into any investment, always remember to do your homework. This not only protects your money, but it gives you the confidence to know that you are making the best decision possible. And, above all, it prepares you to take advantage of opportunities that are truly worthwhile.

The Signs of a Good Investment

Identifying the signs of a good investment is like learning to read a treasure map. These signs are clues that tell you whether the path you are about to take has a real chance of success or whether it is better to look elsewhere. It is not a matter of trusting a "sixth sense," but rather of carefully observing certain indicators that are usually present in a solid investment. Knowing how to recognize these signs helps you make smarter decisions and minimize unnecessary risks.

One of the clearest signs of a good investment is that it has a clear and logical purpose. This means that you fully understand how it works and why it should make a profit. For example, if you are considering investing in a company, you should be able to answer questions like: What problem does this company solve? Why are its products or services needed? If the answer is confusing or unconvincing, that is not a good sign. A good investment always has a solid logic behind it.

Another important sign is the financial strength of the opportunity. If you're considering investing in a business, check its numbers. Does it have a steady stream of income? Are its expenses under control? How high are its debts? A company that consistently generates profits and manages its money well is more likely to be a good investment. If the numbers don't add up or if they seem to rely too much on future promises, you should think twice before investing.

Transparency is another key sign. Good investments don't need to hide information. If someone is offering you an opportunity but seems to avoid answering important questions or presents data in a confusing way, that's a red flag. In contrast, a good investment always presents itself clearly, showing both its strengths and weaknesses. No one can guarantee absolute success, but reliable investments are honest about the risks and potential rewards.

The target market is also a crucial factor. A good investment must be aimed at a real market, one that has sufficient demand to sustain the growth of the business or project. For example, if someone offers to invest in an innovative product that only interests a very small or unengaged audience, that is not an encouraging sign. On the other hand, if the investment is aimed at a large and growing market, that indicates that there is potential to generate profits.

Diversification is another sign to consider. If you're looking at a mutual fund or portfolio, look to see if it's well diversified. A good investment doesn't put all its weight in one industry or asset. Diversifying helps reduce risk because if one sector struggles, others can pick up the slack. If you find an opportunity that relies exclusively on a single product, company or sector, it may be riskier than it seems.

The track record of the project or the people involved is also an important sign. A company or business with a good track record is more likely to offer a solid investment. This doesn't mean that new ideas or companies are bad, but it's easier to trust something that has already demonstrated positive results. If it's an inexperienced team or one with a dubious track record, it's best to do more research before committing your money.

A good investment also usually shows signs of potential growth. This doesn't mean that the project has to be at its peak, but there should be signs that it has room to develop. For example, if you're evaluating a company's stock, look for signs such as increased sales, expansion into new markets, or development of innovative products. If all indications are that the project has reached its limit, it may not be the best option for you.

Another key sign is that the investment has a healthy balance between risk and reward. All investments have a degree of risk, but a good investment should offer rewards that justify those risks. For example, if a project has very high risk but offers low reward, it is best to avoid it. Similarly, if someone promises high returns without risk, be wary. That is a typical sign of something that is too good to be true.

Outside support can also be a valuable indicator. If other experienced investors are interested in the same opportunity, that can be a sign that it's promising. This doesn't mean you should blindly follow the crowd, but it's helpful to know if more experienced people see value in the investment. On the other hand, if it seems like no one else is interested, that can be a warning sign.

Finally, a good investment should align with your own goals and capabilities. Not every opportunity is for everyone. If you are looking for stability, an investment in a volatile market may not be what you need. If you are on a limited budget, you should not commit to something that requires large sums of money up front. The best investment for you will be one that fits your goals, risk tolerance, and current financial situation.

In short, recognizing the signs of a good investment requires attention to detail, patience, and a little common sense. The most attractive opportunities are not always the loudest or most exciting, but those that are backed by facts, logic, and realistic projections. If you take the time to observe these signs and analyze them carefully, you will be in a much stronger position to make decisions that will truly benefit your financial future. And remember, a good investment doesn't just promise you profits, it gives you the peace of mind that comes from knowing you're putting your money into something with solid foundations.

Reading the Numbers

Learning to read numbers is one of the most important skills you need to develop if you want to be a successful investor. Numbers are like the secret language of investing. They tell you the true story of a company, a project, or any opportunity you are considering. Although some people think that analyzing numbers is complicated or boring, the truth is that once you understand the basics, numbers become your best allies in making informed and confident decisions.

The first step in reading numbers is understanding what data is really important. When it comes to investments, not all numbers carry the same weight. For example, if you're evaluating a company, some of the key numbers include revenue, profit, expenses, and debt. This data tells you how the company is doing financially and whether it's on solid footing or struggling to stay afloat. If revenue is growing steadily and debt is under control, that's usually a good sign. But if profits are meager or declining, that's a red flag to investigate further.

Another crucial number is cash flow. This concept may seem technical, but it's actually pretty simple. Cash flow refers to the money coming in and going out of a business or project. It's like checking your personal bank account. If you have more money coming in than you're spending, it means you're in good financial shape. But if you're consistently spending more than you're earning, you're bound to run into trouble sooner or later. In an investment, a positive cash flow is an indicator of stability, while a negative cash flow can be a sign that something isn't right.

Profit margins are another essential number. This metric shows you what percentage of a company's revenue is converted into actual profit. For example, if a company has a profit margin of 20 percent, it means that out of every dollar it earns, 20 cents is profit after all costs are covered. High margins typically indicate efficiency and cost control, while low margins may mean the company is spending too much to generate revenue.

The debt level of a company or project is another factor that you can't ignore. Debt isn't always a bad thing. Many companies take out loans to expand or invest in new projects. However, when debt is too high relative to revenue, it can become a serious problem. A common way to measure this is the debt-to-revenue ratio, which compares how much a company owes to how much it earns. If the ratio is too high, it could mean that the company is at risk if revenue declines.

For those who invest in stocks, another key number is the price-to-earnings ratio, known as P/E. This metric compares a stock's current price to the company's earnings per share. Essentially, it tells you how much investors are willing to pay for each dollar of earnings. If the P/E ratio is too high, it could mean the stock is overvalued. Conversely, a low P/E could indicate the stock is undervalued, though there are always other factors to consider before making a decision.

When it comes to property, the important numbers change a bit, but the principle remains the same. For example, in real estate, you should look at the purchase price, maintenance costs, taxes, and rental income potential. It's also important to consider the resale value and whether the property is in an area that tends to appreciate or depreciate in value over time. If the expected rental income doesn't cover the costs or if the purchase price is too high compared to similar properties, it's probably not a good investment.

Another area where reading numbers is crucial is in new projects or startups. Here, you need to carefully analyze revenue and expense projections. Often, entrepreneurs are optimists by nature and tend to present numbers that seem too good to be true. That's why it's important to look beyond projections and focus on the actual numbers of the present. How much capital do they have? How fast are they burning through their money? How long can they operate with current resources before needing more funding? These questions will help you assess the real risk.

A key point when reading numbers is to avoid falling into the trap of big, flashy numbers. For example, a company may boast millions in revenue, but if its expenses are just as high or higher, that revenue doesn't have much value. You should always look at the bigger picture. Numbers aren't analyzed in isolation; they must be interpreted as a whole to understand the true financial health of an investment.

Finally, don't be afraid to ask for help if the numbers are overwhelming you. Talking to an accountant, financial advisor, or someone with investment experience can make a big difference. They can help you interpret the data and teach you how to spot important patterns. Over time, you'll gain confidence and be able to read the numbers like an expert.

In short, reading numbers is a skill that every investor must master. Numbers are the compass that will guide you through the world of investing, showing you which opportunities have potential and which ones you should avoid. Learning to interpret them will not only protect you from making impulsive decisions, but it will also give you the security of knowing that you are acting with knowledge and logic. And remember, numbers don't lie. You just need to learn to listen to them in order to make smarter financial decisions.

Identifying Scams and Risks

Identifying scams and risks is an essential skill for any investor. In the world of investing, not everything that glitters is gold. Often, scammers and risky projects are presented as incredible opportunities that seem too good to be true – and in fact, they almost always are. That's why it's essential to learn to recognize the warning signs and develop a solid criterion before committing your money to any investment.

The first step in identifying scams is to know the characteristics of a too-perfect offer. If someone promises you guaranteed and exorbitant returns in a short time, that's a big red flag. No legitimate investment can guarantee huge profits without risk. Real investments always have some level of uncertainty, and high rewards often come with higher risks. So, if someone insists there is no risk, be wary immediately.

Another common sign of scams is pressure to make quick decisions. Scammers know that when you have time to think and analyze, you're less likely to fall for their traps. That's why they often use tactics like "this offer is only for today" or "if you don't enter now, you'll miss out on a great opportunity." If someone tries to rush you into investing without giving you time to research, the best thing you can do is walk away.

Lack of transparency is another important indicator. In a legitimate investment, the people responsible for the project are willing to answer all your questions and provide clear information about how the business works. If someone avoids giving you specific details or is evasive, that's a bad sign. Always ask for detailed information, such as financial statements, market research, and background information on the team in charge. If they don't provide it, there's probably something they're trying to hide.

It's vital to research the people behind the investment. Scammers often present themselves as experts or charismatic figures with an impressive track record. However, many times these credentials are fake or exaggerated. Search their name online, verify their work and professional experience, and make sure they really have the necessary knowledge to handle the project. If you can't find reliable information or if their background doesn't match what they say, it's best to stay away.

Another key aspect is to carefully review the legal documents of the investment. Scammers often present contracts full of confusing or ambiguous terms that can hinder your ability to understand what you are actually signing. It is essential to read everything carefully and, if necessary, consult a lawyer or financial advisor. Never invest in something you do not fully understand.

Analyzing the numbers also plays an important role in identifying risks. If the projected returns are much higher than market standards, that is cause for suspicion. You should also analyze how the money is generated in the investment. For example, some fraudulent schemes, such as pyramid schemes, rely on new people investing in order to pay the first participants. If the investment income does not come from a solid business model, but from attracting more investors, you are dealing with a scam.

The internet is a powerful tool for detecting risks. Look for reviews, comments and testimonials about the investment or the people involved. If you find a lot of complaints, warnings or stories of people who have lost money, that should be enough to make you reconsider. There are also scam blacklists in many countries, where you can check if the investment is registered as fraudulent.

Aside from scams, it's important to understand that not all risks come from malicious intent. Sometimes, an investment can be legitimate, but extremely risky. For example, a startup may have a great idea, but if it doesn't have a solid plan to execute it, the odds of failure are high. Analyze the risks inherent in each type of investment and make sure they align with your risk profile and financial goals.

Another type of risk you should consider is liquidity risk. This refers to how easy or difficult it is to convert your investment into cash. Some investments, such as stocks in large companies, are very liquid and can be sold quickly. However, others, such as real estate or long-term projects, may take years to generate a return or be difficult to sell. Make sure you understand how long you might have to tie up your money before you commit.

Finally, develop a healthy skepticism. This doesn't mean you should distrust everyone, but it does mean you should adopt a critical attitude. Always ask yourself: Why is this investment so attractive? What could go wrong? What will I do if things don't go as I expect? Questioning every detail not only protects you from falling for a scam, but it also better prepares you to handle the risks inherent in any investment.

In short, identifying scams and risks requires attention to detail, patience, and a constant commitment to your financial education. Never be afraid to ask questions, seek advice, or reject an offer that seems unclear to you. By protecting yourself from scams and assessing risks objectively, you not only protect your money, but you also give yourself the opportunity to grow as an investor. Always remember that it is better to miss an opportunity than to lose your money on something that was never real.

The Value of the Long Term

The value of the long term is a fundamental concept that every investor must understand and value. In a world where many people seek quick results and immediate profits, stopping to think about what time can do for an investment can make the difference between success and failure. The best opportunities do not always offer instant results, but with patience and vision, the long term can be your greatest ally.

To understand the value of the long term, we must first accept that investing is not a game of chance. When you invest, you are putting your money into a vehicle that needs time to grow, mature, and bear fruit. Whether you are investing in stocks, real estate, a business, or even your own education, true growth does not happen overnight. This growth requires consistency, well-thought-out strategies, and, above all, patience.

Patience over the long term means more than just waiting; it's about resisting the temptation to act impulsively. One of the biggest mistakes new investors make is being carried away by the emotions of the moment. When markets fall, fear drives many to sell their assets at low prices. When markets rise rapidly, greed drives others to buy at inflated prices, hoping to gain more. In both cases, these decisions often hurt investors, because they are not based on the real value of the investment, but on emotional reactions.

A key aspect of long-term value is compound interest, which Albert Einstein once described as the most powerful force in the universe. Compound interest is when your earnings generate more earnings, and those additional earnings generate more earnings. Over time, this effect can transform a modest initial investment into something significant. But for compound interest to work in your favor, you need to give it time. Without the long-term perspective, this effect loses its power.

Another important benefit of long-term investing is that it allows you to take advantage of stability. Over short time frames, markets tend to be volatile. They frequently rise and fall due to news, rumors, or unexpected events. However, over long time frames, these fluctuations tend to smooth out, and real growth trends become more apparent. This means that by holding an investment for a long period, you are more likely to see a positive return, even if there are ups and downs along the way.

The long term also allows you to evaluate an investment's performance more objectively. Instead of worrying about daily price changes, you can focus on the fundamentals of what you're investing in. For example, if you invest in a company, you can look at its revenue growth, its ability to innovate, and its position in the market, rather than worrying about how its stock price fluctuates from day to day. This perspective helps you make more informed, less impulsive decisions.

One factor that is often overlooked is that investing for the long term protects you from the hidden costs associated with constantly moving your investments. Every time you buy or sell an asset, there are costs involved, such as commissions, taxes, and price spreads. These costs, while seemingly small, can quickly add up if you make too many moves in a short period of time.

Holding your investments for longer reduces these costs, allowing you to retain more of your profits.

Investing with the long term in mind also has a positive emotional component. Instead of constantly worrying about daily ups and downs, you can relax and trust your strategy. Knowing that you have a solid plan and are focused on future goals can reduce stress and allow you to make clearer, more effective decisions. Plus, this approach helps you develop discipline and patience, qualities that are essential not just for investing, but for life in general.

Another aspect of the value of the long term is that it allows you to take advantage of opportunities that many people overlook. When the overall focus is on quick wins, many investors ignore projects or assets that take time to develop but have enormous potential. By taking a long-term perspective, you can identify and take advantage of these opportunities before they become obvious to others.

Finally, it's important to remember that long-term doesn't mean just putting your money away and forgetting about it. While patience is key, you also need to monitor your investments periodically and make sure they're still aligned with your goals. The market, industries, and your personal goals can change over time, and it's essential to adjust your strategy when necessary. However, these adjustments should be made strategically and not in response to temporary fluctuations.

In conclusion, the value of the long term lies in the ability to let time work in your favor. It is a strategy that requires confidence, patience, and commitment, but the benefits can be immense. By focusing on the future and resisting the temptation to seek immediate results, you are building a path to wealth and financial stability. Remember that investing is not a sprint, but a marathon. Those who understand the power of the long term not only achieve higher returns, but also enjoy a smoother and more satisfying process.

Don't Put All Your Eggs in One Basket

Don't put all your eggs in one basket is one of the most well-known rules in the investment world, and for good reason. This metaphor teaches us the importance of diversification, which is nothing more than spreading the risk across different areas instead of concentrating it all in one option. If you've ever wondered why it's so crucial to follow this practice, the answer lies in common sense: if the basket falls and all the eggs are in the same place, you're likely to lose them all. But if you spread them across several baskets, even if one falls, the others will be safe.

When it comes to investing, the mistake of concentrating all your money on a single asset, industry or market can be devastating. No matter how promising an investment may seem, there is always the possibility that something can go wrong. A seemingly solid company may face an unexpected crisis, a market may suffer a crash or a technology may become obsolete faster than we imagine. Diversification acts as insurance against these unexpected events, minimizing the impact of a potential loss.

Diversifying doesn't just mean investing in a bunch of random things. It's a strategic process that requires analyzing and selecting different assets that aren't directly related to each other. For example, if you decide to invest only in technology companies, even though you're diversifying within the sector, you're still exposed to the same general risks of that industry. However, if you combine investments in technology with others in real estate, government bonds, or commodities like gold, you're creating a more balanced portfolio. The idea is that if one of these areas faces problems, the others can compensate for it.

Another reason to diversify is that different types of investments tend to behave differently at specific times. For example, when stock markets are down, bonds are often a more stable option. Similarly, real estate can offer a steady source of income even during times of economic uncertainty. By holding a variety of assets, you're building a portfolio that can better withstand the natural ups and downs of the economy.

It's important to understand that diversifying also means thinking geographically. Many people limit their investments to the country where they live, which can be a mistake if the local economy is struggling. Investing in international markets allows you to take advantage of growth in other parts of the world and protect yourself against fluctuations in a specific economy. For example, while one region may be facing a recession, another could be booming.

Diversification applies not only to what type of assets you choose, but also to how you allocate your resources within each category. If you decide to invest in stocks, don't put all your money into one company, no matter how successful it seems. Instead, consider investing in several companies in different sectors. The same goes for real estate; don't buy all your properties in the same city or even the same type of property. The more differences there are between your investments, the lower the risk that they will all suffer at the same time.

A common mistake new investors make is underestimating the need to diversify when they are starting out with little capital. The idea that you need a lot of money to diversify is a myth. Today, there are tools like mutual funds and index funds that allow you to invest in a wide range of assets even with a small amount of money. These options are great for those who want to diversify without overcomplicating things.

Despite all the benefits of diversification, it's important not to take it to extremes. If you spread your money out too far, you could end up with a portfolio that's unwieldy and doesn't generate significant returns. Balance is key. Diversify enough to reduce risk, but not so much that you lose focus or dilute your gains too much.

Another important point when diversifying is to regularly monitor your portfolio. Market conditions change over time, and what initially seemed like a solid mix of investments may need adjusting. This doesn't mean you should be constantly moving your money around, but you should periodically review how your assets are performing and make changes when necessary.

Not putting all your eggs in one basket also means having a clear plan for your money. Diversification isn't a guarantee of success, but it does increase your chances of protecting yourself against significant losses. By doing so, you're creating a stronger foundation for your finances, giving you peace of mind and more options in the long run.

Finally, remember that diversifying not only protects your money, but also your peace of mind. Knowing that you are not betting everything on one option allows you to sleep better at night, even when the markets are volatile. This peace of mind is priceless and is one of the biggest benefits of spreading your investments wisely. If you understand and apply this rule, you will be taking a big step towards becoming a wiser and more prepared investor.

The Role of Trends and Context

The role of trends and context in the world of investing is something that cannot be ignored if you really want to make informed decisions and increase your chances of success. A trend is nothing more than a direction in which something is moving, while context is the environment in which that trend is developing. Both factors are key because they help you understand not only where a market, sector or asset is heading, but also why it is doing so.

Trends are like waves in the ocean. They can be big and long-lasting or small and fleeting. Some are very clear and easy to identify, while others are more subtle and require a trained eye to spot. For example, the rise of renewable energy is a trend that has been developing for years and looks set to continue growing due to growing concern for the environment. If you decide to invest in this sector, you are likely riding a wave that still has a long way to go. On the other hand, some trends, such as certain technological fads or viral phenomena, can disappear as quickly as they came, leaving investors stranded if they do not react in time.

Understanding context is just as important. It's not enough to know that something is trendy or booming; you need to understand what's driving it. Context includes factors such as the global economy, government policies, technological advancements, cultural shifts, and even weather events. For example, the rise of electric vehicles isn't just because the technology is exciting, but also because many governments are offering incentives for their adoption and people are increasingly interested in reducing their environmental impact. If you ignore these factors, you could overestimate or underestimate the potential of an investment.

To take advantage of trends and context, you first need to develop the ability to observe what's happening around you. This includes reading the news, following industry experts, and paying attention to changes in people's behaviors. If you notice that more and more people are using electric bikes in your city, you might want to investigate whether this trend is local or global. If you find that major manufacturers are investing in this technology, it's probably a trend with growth potential.

Another key aspect is to differentiate between a fad and a true trend. Fads are often fleeting and driven more by the hype of the moment than by solid fundamentals. An example might be the rise of certain cryptocurrencies that appear out of nowhere, generate a lot of media buzz, and then quickly lose value. A solid trend, on the other hand, is based on deeper, more sustainable changes, such as the digitalization of business or the aging of the population in many parts of the world.

Context also includes understanding the risks associated with a trend. For example, investing in technology can be very profitable during a period of economic growth, but in a recession, tech companies are often the first to face cutbacks. Knowing the overall state of the economy and how it might affect your investments is crucial to avoid unpleasant surprises. If you don't take context into account, you could end up investing in something that looked promising, but was actually doomed from the start due to external circumstances.

Plus, context helps you make more strategic decisions. Imagine you've identified a growing trend, such as the mass adoption of remote work. If you understand that this trend is supported by a cultural shift toward better work-life balance, you can look for opportunities at companies that make home office furniture, video conferencing platforms, or even productivity apps. By knowing the full picture, you're better equipped to identify related opportunities that others might miss.

A common mistake is trying to anticipate trends without having enough information. Many people jump into investing in something simply because they heard it was hot, without taking the time to understand why. This approach almost always leads to bad decisions. Patience and analysis are your best allies. If a trend is really strong and backed by a solid context, you will have time to get into it after doing your research thoroughly.

Another important point is that not all trends are suitable for all investors. Some require more capital, more time or more risk tolerance. For example, investing in startups can be very profitable, but it is also extremely risky because many of them fail. If your investor profile is more conservative, you may prefer to focus on safer trends, such as investing in established companies that are adapting to a new context.

Finally, never forget that both trends and context can change. What seems like a great opportunity today may lose momentum in the future if the environment changes. That's why it's essential to review your investments regularly and always stay informed about what's happening in the world. Stay flexible and willing to adjust your strategy if conditions require it. Adapting to change is one of the most important skills you can develop as an investor.

Understanding the role of trends and context not only helps you find better opportunities, but it also protects you from falling into traps. By analyzing each investment with a broad and detailed view, you will be much better prepared to make decisions that actually make sense and can lead you to achieve your financial goals.

Timing in Investments

Timing in investing is an essential concept that, when properly understood, can make the difference between success and failure. It basically refers to the moment when you decide to enter or exit an investment. Although it may seem like a simple thing, timing is a combination of analysis, patience, and sometimes a bit of intuition. It is not just about buying low and selling high, but doing so at the right time, which requires a good understanding of the market and the factors that affect it.

To start, it is important to understand that timing is everything in the world of investing. Financial markets, real estate, commodities, or any other asset you may consider investing in are constantly moving. These movements are driven by a number of factors, such as supply and demand, changes in economic policies, investor emotions, and global news. The goal of good timing is to take advantage of these movements to maximize your profits and minimize your risks.

A common mistake that many people make is trying to guess the perfect time to invest. This is known as trying to "timing" the market, and while it sounds tempting, in practice it is extremely difficult. No one has a crystal ball to accurately predict the future. Even the most experienced investors can get it wrong. What you can do instead is identify patterns and signals that tell you when it is a good time to act.

For example, if you're considering investing in stocks, looking at historical market performance can give you valuable clues. Markets often move in cycles, alternating between growth and correction phases. Buying during a correction, when prices are lower, can be a smart strategy, as long as the asset in question has solid fundamentals. However, this doesn't mean you should jump in right away just because something is cheap. Sometimes a low price can indicate deeper problems in the company or sector, so you should always do your research before making a decision.

In the case of real estate, timing is also crucial. Here, factors such as interest rates, the supply of properties on the market, and general economic trends play an important role. For example, during an economic downturn, property prices often fall because there are fewer active buyers. This can be a good time to buy, especially if you have a long-term view. However, you should also consider how long you are willing to wait for the market to recover and prices to rise again.

Another aspect of timing is knowing when to exit an investment. Many people hold on to their assets for too long, hoping they will rise in price even further, only to see the market turn around and lose their gains. This is where the importance of having a clear strategy from the start comes into play. Before investing, define your goals and set limits. Decide how much you are willing to make before selling and how much you are willing to lose before cutting your losses. These decisions should be based on data and not emotion.

Timing is also related to your investment horizon. If you are investing for the short term, as in the case of trading, the exact moment of entry and exit is much more critical. Here, every market movement counts, and you will need to constantly keep an eye on fluctuations. On the other hand, if your horizon is long-term, as in the case of index funds or real estate, small daily or even monthly changes matter less. In these cases, it is more important to focus on the overall trends and fundamentals of the asset.

Another key point of timing is to avoid panic or euphoria. When markets are booming, it is easy to get excited and buy for fear of missing out. This is known as the FOMO effect. Similarly, when markets are falling, fear can lead you to sell at the worst possible time. The key is to stay calm and make decisions based on rational analysis and not emotions.

To improve your timing, you can use tools such as technical analysis, which studies price and volume charts to identify patterns and trends. You can also rely on fundamental analysis, which examines financial and economic data to assess whether an asset is overvalued or undervalued. Both approaches have their advantages and limitations, and combining them can give you a more complete perspective.

Finally, remember that perfect timing doesn't exist. Even if you take all the precautions and do all the right things, there will always be an element of uncertainty. The market is unpredictable and influenced by factors that are often beyond your control. The important thing is to learn from your experiences and adjust your strategy as you go.

In short, investment timing is not about guessing the future, but about making informed decisions at the right time. This involves observing the market, understanding the cycles, defining your goals, and acting with discipline. By doing so, you will not only increase your chances of success, but you will also reduce the stress that often comes with the world of investing. With time and practice, you will develop a better intuition for knowing when it is time to act and when it is better to wait.

When and How to Seek Help

Seeking help is an essential part of the investing process, and in general, of handling any major financial decision. Sometimes, it's hard to recognize when we need support, either because we think we can handle everything on our own or because we're afraid of appearing inexperienced by asking for help. However, seeking guidance at the right time can be the difference between making an informed decision and making a costly mistake.

The first step in knowing when to seek help is to recognize your limitations. No one knows everything, and that's okay. If you feel like you don't fully understand an investment-related topic, such as financial analysis, market projections, or tax implications, that's a clear sign that you need help. This isn't a sign of weakness, but rather of intelligence. Most successful investors don't work alone; they have a network of experts who advise them in areas where they don't have enough experience.

Another sign that it's time to seek help is when you feel overwhelmed by the amount of information available. In the world of investing, data is everywhere: economic news, expert analysis, social media opinions, and endless charts. If you can't process it all effectively or don't know how to distinguish between useful information and noise, a financial advisor can be a great ally. They can help you filter out the important stuff and focus your attention on what really matters.

Fear and uncertainty are other indicators that you need to seek help. It's normal to feel hesitant before making a financial decision, especially if it involves a significant amount of money. But if fear is paralyzing you and you can't move forward, talking to someone more experienced can help you clarify your thoughts and make a more relaxed decision. Sometimes, you just need someone to confirm that you're on the right track or point out something you hadn't considered.

A common situation where seeking help is crucial is when you are faced with complex or unfamiliar investments. For example, if you are considering entering a foreign market, investing in cryptocurrencies, or participating in a business that has multiple unknown variables, an expert in the area can offer you a clearer perspective. Reading about a topic is not the same as having someone who lives it day-to-day explain the pros and cons to you.

Now, not all forms of help are created equal, and knowing how to look for it is also important. The first step is to identify the type of help you need. If you're looking for general advice on how to manage your personal finances, a financial advisor may be sufficient. If you're interested in a specific type of investment, such as real estate or stocks, look for someone with direct experience in that field. On the other hand, if you need technical help, such as understanding the legal or tax aspects of an investment, a specialized lawyer or accountant might be the best options.

Once you know what kind of help you need, do your research on who to turn to. Not everyone who presents themselves as an expert has the necessary credentials. Look for references, check their experience, and if possible, talk to others who have worked with them before. For financial advisors, check to see if they are certified and have a proven track record of success. This is especially important if you are paying for their services, as you want to make sure you are getting value for your money.

Also, don't underestimate the power of informal networks. Talking to friends, family, or colleagues who have experience in investing can be a free and valuable way to gain information. Sometimes, the people closest to you can offer practical advice based on their own experience. However, remember that their recommendations are based on their specific situation, which might not be the same as yours. Always take their advice as a reference, not a definitive guide.

Another key aspect of seeking help is being willing to listen and learn. There's no point in asking for advice if you're not open to considering new ideas or changing your approach. Often, pride or stubbornness can prevent you from making the most of the guidance offered. Remember that the goal of seeking help is to improve your decisions and, ultimately, your results.

It's also important to set clear boundaries with your advisor. While you can rely on their expertise, you should never completely delegate your decisions. You are ultimately responsible for your investments, and it's crucial that you understand what you're doing. Help should be a tool to improve your knowledge and confidence, not a crutch to avoid responsibility.

Finally, keep in mind that seeking help isn't a one-time thing. As you grow as an investor, you'll face new challenges and situations that will require different types of support. The world of investing is constantly changing, and keeping an open mind to learn from others is one of the best ways to adapt and thrive.

In short, seeking help at the right time and in the right way is an essential skill for any investor. It's not about admitting weakness, but about demonstrating intelligence and prudence. By acknowledging your limitations, doing your research, and staying open-minded, you can ensure that the support you receive propels you toward your financial goals, not derails you from your path.

Tools for the Modern Investor

The world of investing has changed dramatically in recent decades, and the modern investor has a wealth of tools at their disposal that can make the difference between making well-informed decisions or acting blindly. These tools not only facilitate access to valuable information, but also allow it to be analyzed effectively, which is crucial to maximizing opportunities and minimizing risks. Knowing and taking advantage of these tools can be a turning point in your path as an investor.

One of the most important tools for any modern investor is a trading platform. These platforms allow you to buy and sell assets such as stocks, bonds, cryptocurrencies, and more. There are many options on the market, and it is important to choose one that fits your needs and level of experience. For example, some platforms are designed for beginners, with simple interfaces and educational tools, while others offer advanced features such as detailed charts and automated trading options for more experienced investors. Before choosing a platform, research its costs, ease of use, and the variety of assets available.

Another essential tool is financial analysis software. These programs allow you to evaluate the performance of different assets and understand their behavior over time. With them, you can create graphs, calculate financial ratios, and simulate what-if scenarios. Good analysis software can help you identify patterns in data that would not be obvious to the naked eye. Some examples include programs specialized in technical analysis, which focus on market trends, and others focused on fundamental analysis, which evaluate the financial health of a company or asset.

Mobile apps are also a great tool for the modern investor. We live in a world where opportunities can arise at any time, and having access to up-to-date information from your phone can make a huge difference. Many of these apps allow you to monitor markets in real-time, set price alerts, and receive relevant news instantly. Plus, some even include interactive learning features, making them ideal for those just starting out in the world of investing.

Research tools are also essential. There are online services that offer you detailed reports on different assets, industries, and market trends. These reports are often prepared by professional analysts and can provide you with deeper insight into the opportunities and risks associated with certain investments. Some services even allow you to customize your preferences to receive specific recommendations based on your interests and goals.

Additionally, financial calculators are a basic but extremely useful tool. These calculators allow you to estimate everything from expected returns to the impact of taxes or compound interest on your investments. While many trading platforms include built-in calculators, you can also find free online tools that serve this purpose effectively.

We cannot forget social media and investor communities. Although you should be careful with the quality of information in these spaces, online communities can be a great way to learn from other investors, share experiences and keep up to date with market trends. Platforms such as Twitter, Reddit or specialized forums are often the place where interesting conversations arise and ideas are shared that can be the starting point for your research.

Another valuable resource is portfolio management tools. These apps help you keep an organized record of your investments, including gains, losses, and changes in the value of your assets. Good portfolio management is key to evaluating the overall performance of your investments and making adjustments when necessary. Additionally, these tools often offer detailed reports that allow you to identify areas for improvement in your strategy.

For investors interested in more complex investments, such as real estate or startups, there are specific platforms designed to facilitate access to these opportunities. For example, in real estate, you can find sites that allow you to invest in properties with small amounts of money through crowdfunding models. In the case of startups, crowdfunding platforms give you access to innovative projects with growth potential. These tools have democratized access to investments that were previously reserved for large capitals.

Finally, we cannot talk about tools for the modern investor without mentioning artificial intelligence and machine learning. These technologies are revolutionizing the way we analyze and understand the markets. There are programs that use advanced algorithms to predict market movements, identify behavioral patterns, and even automate transactions. Although these tools still require human supervision, they can save time and improve the accuracy of decision making.

In short, the modern investor has access to a wide variety of tools that make every step of the investment process easier. From trading platforms and analysis software to mobile apps and portfolio management tools, technology is at your fingertips to help you invest smarter. The real challenge is learning how to use these tools effectively, integrating them into your investment strategy and using them to support informed decision-making. If you can do that, you'll be one step closer to achieving your financial goals.

What to Learn from the Best

Learning from the best is a smart strategy in any area of life, but in the world of investing it is practically essential. Great investors are not only successful because of their results, but because of the principles and strategies that got them there. They have faced the same challenges as any beginner, but they have known how to turn mistakes into lessons and take advantage of opportunities like no one else. Knowing what the best have to teach can not only save you time and money, but also help you avoid unnecessary pitfalls.

One of the key lessons you can learn from top investors is the importance of patience. Figures like Warren Buffett have shown that successful investments are not always those that seek quick gains, but those that allow time to work its magic. Patience does not mean inaction, but rather making well-thought-out decisions and giving them the time they need to bear fruit. For example, rather than trying to guess short-term market movements, many great investors prefer to focus on assets that have long-term potential, allowing compound interest and natural market growth to do their work.

Another key aspect that the best investors emphasize is the importance of research. No matter how long they have been investing or how many resources they have at their disposal, they don't make decisions without doing a thorough analysis first. This means studying the numbers, understanding the economic context, knowing the risks, and making sure that an opportunity really aligns with their goals. Research not only gives you clarity, but it also allows you to invest with confidence, knowing that you are relying on solid information and not hunches.

Furthermore, great investors usually have a clear focus on diversification. They understand that no investment is completely safe, and that is why they never risk everything on a single asset or sector. This strategy not only protects their capital, but also allows them to take advantage of opportunities in different areas of the market. Diversification is like insurance: it may not make you rich overnight, but it definitely reduces the likelihood of devastating losses.

One trait that the best investors share is the ability to manage their emotions. The market can be extremely volatile, and making decisions based on fear or greed often leads to costly mistakes. The best investors know how to stay calm even in times of crisis, assessing situations objectively rather than reacting impulsively. Learning to manage your emotions will not only protect your money, but also your peace of mind, which is just as important in the long run.

Humility is another key lesson great investors teach us. No matter how successful they are, they know they can't predict the future or get every decision right. This leads them to be cautious, listen to different perspectives, and be willing to admit when they're wrong. Humility allows you to constantly learn, adapt to changes, and grow as an investor. Conversely, arrogance can lead you to ignore warning signs and take unnecessary risks.

Something that also stands out among the best is their willingness to learn from mistakes. They don't see losses as failures, but rather as learning opportunities. Every mistake contains a valuable lesson about what works and what doesn't. Instead of blaming the market or external factors, great investors analyze their decisions and look for ways to improve. This approach not only improves your skills, but also prepares you to face future challenges with more confidence and wisdom.

Another aspect worth highlighting is the long-term approach that many great investors have. They don't get distracted by fads or passing market trends. Instead, they look for assets that offer real, sustainable value over time. This can mean investing in companies with solid fundamentals, real estate in strategic locations, or even innovative projects with growth potential. Their mindset is based on building wealth steadily and sustainably, rather than seeking immediate gains that can disappear just as quickly.

Finally, the best also teach us the importance of surrounding ourselves with smart people. No one has all the answers, and having a good team or even trusted mentors can make a big difference. This includes everything from financial advisors to colleagues who share your interest in learning and improving. Investing doesn't have to be a lonely path, and working with others can give you access to knowledge, perspectives, and opportunities that you might not have found on your own.

Learning from the best doesn't mean copying them, but rather understanding their principles and adapting them to your own situation. Every investor has a unique background, with different goals, resources, and risk tolerance. However, the principles of patience, research, diversification, emotional control, humility, constant learning, long-term focus, and teamwork are applicable to anyone who wants to invest successfully. By incorporating these lessons into your own strategy, you'll be building a solid foundation for achieving your financial goals and becoming the kind of investor others will one day want to emulate.

Steps to Get Started Today

Getting started with investing can seem complicated, but the key is to take the first steps in a conscious and organized manner. You don't need to be an expert to get started today; all you need is to be willing to learn and take action. Every decision you make will bring you closer to your financial goals. Here I will guide you through the basic steps so you can start your journey as an investor.

The first step is to understand your financial goals. Before investing, you should ask yourself what you hope to achieve with your money. Do you want to save for retirement, buy a house, build an emergency fund, or simply grow your wealth? Being clear about your goals will help you define how long you can let your money work, what kind of risks you can take, and what kind of investments best suit your needs. This point is essential because without a clear objective, it is easy to lose direction and make impulsive decisions.

The second step is to analyze your current financial situation. You can't afford to invest money that you need to cover your basic expenses or pay off high-interest debts. Make a budget and make sure your finances are in order. If you have outstanding debts, especially those with high interest rates, it's best to prioritize them before investing. Once you have an emergency fund, which usually amounts to three to six months of your basic expenses, you'll be in a better position to start investing with peace of mind.

The third step is to educate yourself about the investment options available. This doesn't mean you need to become an expert overnight, but you should take the time to understand the basics. Learn what stocks, bonds, mutual funds, real estate, and other alternatives are. Familiarize yourself with terms like diversification, return on investment, and risk tolerance. There are many free resources available, from books to online videos, that can help you get started.

The fourth step is to decide how much you are willing to invest. This is a critical point because you need to start with an amount that won't put you in a difficult financial situation. Many investment platforms allow you to start with small amounts, so you don't need to be a millionaire to get started. However, set a monthly amount that you can allocate consistently. This discipline is what will make the difference in the long run.

The fifth step is to choose a platform or broker to invest with. Nowadays, there are a lot of options, from mobile apps to traditional banks and online brokers. When choosing one, make sure it is reliable, easy to use, and suitable for your level of experience. Research their fees, the investment options they offer, and reviews from other users. If it's your first time, look for a platform that offers educational tools and technical support to help you through the process.

Step six is to start small and diversify. Don't try to bet all your capital on one investment in the hopes of making big profits quickly. Instead, spread your money across different options to reduce risk. For example, if you're investing in stocks, don't buy just one company. If you're starting out with mutual funds, choose one that invests in different sectors. This approach will protect you from significant losses and allow you to learn without putting all your money at risk.

The seventh step is to keep learning and adjusting your strategy. Once you've started, it doesn't mean the job is done. Spend time reviewing the performance of your investments, stay informed about market trends, and adjust your strategy as needed. Don't be afraid to make changes if something isn't working, but avoid making decisions based solely on emotions. Investing is a constant process of learning and improvement.

The eighth step is to be patient and consistent. Investing is not a quick game, and the results are not always immediate. Many people get discouraged because they expect to see big profits in a short time, but the reality is that most investments take time to mature. Patience, combined with a clear strategy and the discipline to continue investing regularly, is what will lead you to success.

Finally, the ninth step is to not be afraid to seek help when you need it. If you feel overwhelmed or unsure, consult a financial advisor or join communities where you can learn from the experience of other investors. Investing doesn't have to be a lonely path, and having the support of more experienced people can make a big difference.

Getting started today doesn't mean you have to know everything or need a lot of money. It means taking small steps that will bring you closer to your goals and allow you to build the habit of investing. The most important thing is to take action. Every day you put off your decision is a day your money could be working for you. With clarity, discipline, and education, you can begin to build a stronger financial future and achieve your goals. All you need to do is take that first step.

www.ingramcontent.com/pod-product-compliance
Lightning Source LLC
Chambersburg PA
CBHW021112130726
47988CB00003B/992